AN ELEGY FOR
THE GALOSHERMAN

Also by Matt Simpson

Letters to Berlin (Driftwood Publications, 1971)
A Skye Sequence (Driftwood Publications, 1972)
Watercolour from an Approved School (Toulouse Press, 1975)
Uneasy Vespers (Windows, 1977)
Making Arrangements (Bloodaxe Books, 1982)
See You on the Christmas Tree (Windows, 1984)
Dead Baiting (Four Eyes Press, 1989)

An Elegy for the Galosherman

NEW & SELECTED POEMS

MATT SIMPSON

BLOODAXE BOOKS

Copyright © Matt Simpson 1982, 1984, 1989, 1990

ISBN: 1 85224 103 9

First published 1990 by
Bloodaxe Books Ltd,
P.O. Box 1SN,
Newcastle upon Tyne NE99 1SN.

Bloodaxe Books Ltd acknowledges
the financial assistance of Northern Arts.

Typesetting by Bryan Williamson, Darwen, Lancashire.

Printed in Great Britain by
Billing & Sons Limited, Worcester.

For Monika, David, Catherine

Acknowledgements

Forty-three of these poems were published in *Making Arrangements* (Bloodaxe Books, 1982). That collection was dedicated to Norman Nicholson.

Acknowledgements are due to the editors of the following publications in which versions of some of these poems have appeared: *Brando's Hat, The Burton Collection, Critical Quarterly, Critical Survey, Divan, The Echo Room, Encounter, English, The Fitzwilliam Magazine, The Green Book, Here Now, Honest Ulsterman, Iron, Lancashire Life, The Literary Review, London Magazine, London Review of Books, The New Review, 051, Outposts, Phoenix, Poetry Merseyside, Poetry Nottingham, Poetry Review, Poetry Voice, Poetry Wales, Quarto, Smoke, Stork Talk, Stride, The Times Literary Supplement* and *Ventilator*.

Some have also been published in the following books: *Between Comets: for Norman Nicholson at 70* (Taxus, 1984), *Me, Myself, I* (Mary Glasgow, 1985), *New Poetry 2* (Arts Council, 1976), *Poetry With an Edge* (Bloodaxe Books, 1988), *Shrieking Silence* (Scarecrow Press, New Jersey, 1988), *The Least Thing* (Stride, 1989), *The Poetry Show: 2* (Macmillan, 1989), and *Toughie Toffee* (Collins, 1989).

Versions of four of the poems here were published in the pamphlet, *See You on the Christmas Tree* (Windows, 1984) and the sequence *Dead Baiting* was published as a pamphlet by Four Eyes Press in 1989. 'After Such Knowledge' was included in a collection of poems presented to Geoffrey Holloway on his seventieth birthday.

Some of the poems have been broadcast by BBC Radio Merseyside and Radio City.

The cover photograph by Shirley Baker is taken from her book *Street Photographs* (Bloodaxe Books, 1989).

Contents

DEAD BAITING

It matters only in
So far as we want to be telling

Each other alive about each other
Alive.

W.S. GRAHAM

Every man thinks meanly of himself for not
having been a soldier, or not having been at sea.

SAMUEL JOHNSON

Directions

With a war to forget, we grew up
on what was left of something, weeds
on battered ground where houses once had stood:

plantain tough as boots, irascible dock,
dogged dandelion, and come-up-smiling rose-
bay willow-herb among strewn bricks;

streets of tar and cobble
with dusty corner shops
and lamp-posts you could swing on –

ropes that smelt of creosote and ships:
a centripetal spin into a vicious hug of iron,
a centrifugal jerk to outer space.

An Elegy for the Galosherman

Who pads the Bowles Street jigger now?
Who's pacing there on noiseless soles
breathing the bad-blood darkness in
between the sleeping back-to-backs?

Was it a dull bull-headed thing
betrayed by its own strength that chafed
the backyard walls? Or some
bewildered sad old man
who wished to keep the darkness clean?

ALL AT 231

They are begging us, you see, in their wordless way,
To do something, to speak on their behalf
Or at least not to close the door again.
            DEREK MAHON

My Grandmother's African Grey

My father's brother brought it home,
madcap Cliff, a 'case', with wit as wild
as erotic dreams. It was his proof
of Africa and emblem of the family pride
in seamanship.
                    But the parrot quickly sensed
our pride was ragged. Perverse, it
nipped its feathers out
with tar-black pincering beak, until,
baring a stubbly breast, it looked
like poultry obscenely undead.

A gift to grandma and to Auntie Bell
who lived together, two odd shoes
inside a wardrobe of a house, it learnt
to parody my grandma's Liverpudlian
wash-house talk, her lovely common-
as-muck, which it counterpointed faithfully
with Auntie Bell's posh how-d'you-do's
that froze you to politeness:
Sunday Best, with little finger cocked.

The bird survived them both, lost all sense
of Africa, one quarter of a century on a perch.
Shabby slate-grey feathers came to mean
my grandmother; its tail's red splash
was Auntie Bell – their stout and brandy accents
jangling on inside the cage.

Territorials: Grandma

In the eye of Florrie's front garden
peppery-throated lilies grow,
loudspeakerfuls of sobering hymns
and mustering drums which at a flick
can swamp the Sodom-and-Gomorrah streets
with God's Own Light...

Tread softly, moggies of Other Persuasions
who'd drill your acids in her soil.

Nerve Centre

The eye swilling in a pyrex saucer
is grandad's. His magnifying glass
is on reconnaissance, zooms above
battlegrounds, in and out of flak.

Collarless shirt, unlaced pumps,
sticking-plastered specs – hums, ha's,
contriving rescue of a son
torpedoed, captured, held

behind barbed Stalag wires; plots
gratifying moves across
a *Daily Telegraph* wall map;
punctures Europe with little flags

on pins. In the gaslit kitchen
a mangle is trundling, the rack
above the bath hangs heavy,
a cast-iron kettle rushes steam.

Stewardess: Bella

Tanners on Sundays,
Christmases two bob:

the boy-myself
braving a maiden
great-aunt's wart
and spiv-fringed lip
sooty as the hob
she smoked in front of
cursing slow kettles,
sagging coals
that hissed to her
tossed butts.

A dragged-out
cremation of a life
they said had looked
on better days.

I poked embers
for visions –
flatulent bandsmen
oompah-oompahing,
three-, four-funnellers
cheered out of town,
streamered with
happiest returns,
gently smoking away.

All Clear

It's time to scrub the sky
clean of enemies
and vigilance,
                    sirens,
searchlights,
the pom-pom-pom
of flak;
          time
to knead and bake,
set jelly on
the window-sill,
jam trestled streets
with kids,
                    let flags
jangle.

          In
Florrie's back garden
the may bush sings
of marzipan,
                    confetti hugs
the air raid shelter;
                         time
to cope with aftermaths
and welcomings –
                    white
petal litterings
excited in the wind.

Crazy Paving

Straddling cracks, each foot on an island,
the small boy, bewildered, sulks down at his shoes,
brand-new and blue as the all-clear sky.
He is not grateful the war is over.
Look up, smile, someone is bullying.

Later they snap his home-from-sea father,
scraping the leavings of milk-rice and nutmeg,
playing the softie, licking the spoon.

The boy has retreated into the house.
It smells of bird seed, peelings and slops.
The draining-board's scrubbed soft as a moth.

Outside there's laughter.
But where are the bluebirds? Is this tomorrow
when the world's free?

Off the Back of a Lorry: Cliff

Uncle humping spuds
grabbing sacks by the ears
like pigs   all hock
and hoof
          lobbed
a blood orange
thudding in my pram

Nit Nurse came
to scratch the muck of war
from tattyheads

Uncle kept his mind
and face in shadow
refused
the handshakes
of the street

forbidden fruit
had swelled up
hooflike
on his brow

I stumbled in shadow
grabbing whispers
by the ears   words
more secret than cupboards

that stunned
like cracked down
rifle butts
flexed my body
like a fist

After Grandad's Funeral

A sideboard feared –
    hefty muscles bronzed,
    oiled, he-man torso
    rippling.

Aboard, a bowl, wax fruit
    hated now – refusing
    to moulder, trashy
    Carmen Miranda grin.

A silver bullet, clean
    top C I aimed –
    pure hysteric scream
    straight between the teeth.

A Face-Lift

Not the house I knew.
No orange lilies'
flagrant fealty.
No elder bush
stripped for its marshmallow pith
to squeeze between
the finger and the thumb
like a fat bogie.
Something has been traded in.
New sills
a mint-cake white
and pebble-dash as fresh
as apple crumble
now propose another pride
from iron-and-coal's
this house
had settled on.
And this house had
a sense of it.
Blunt wisdoms foundered
long before
workmen levered out
its hob and heart.
Here, knowing that the dreams we use
to coddle us all fail,
my grandmother
knelt down
on her cold kitchen's stone
and in the oven gently plumped
a cushion for her head.

*   *   *

Who's Who in Bootle
(for Philip Gardner)

Whoever named the streets where I grew up
must have been a simple-minded philanthrope
who wished brave things on Working Men,
or some at-a-loss committee man
who knew a bright librarian.

A grand eccentric pantheon
of poets and of novelists was where I lived,
illustrious names that no one knew
and some, like Cow-per, mispronounced.

Dryden, Pope, and Akenside,
Prior, Smollett, Bowles, and Keats.
But who the hell was Falconer? And who
were Beattie, Armstrong? Eliot, of course,
was only George. And now I know
who Bulwer was (where our house stood):
a dandy lord who wrote of Pompeii's Last Days.
He should have been here for the Blitz.

The curfew tolled at Gray Street school
each nine a.m.; but the Gray was adjectival.
And Norton Street – I suppose was one of *Gorboduc*
(but where was Sackville?) – saw the start
of my romances and cute eventual tragedies
with choirgirls from St Leonard's Church.

It was under a lamp in Prior Street
that poets started mattering (like sex).
From a library book my Best Friend read
a wanton and corrupting thing:
'Or...through the paddler's bowl/Sailed up the sun.'
It sounded wild iambic gongs across grey roofs.
And Tennyson, Waller, Kipling, and Scott,
Moore, and Gower, and all the rest,
like Rip Van Winkles, rubbed their eyes.

Making Arrangements

Look at the map. The streets where I grew up
move in a direction hard to resist,
lines of force that drag down to grey docks,
to where my father spent his strength.

I am making these arrangements into meaning
to re-inhabit after twenty years some places of
myself – backyards full of ships and cranes,
of hard-knock talk, and death – not just
to mouth at ghosts, unless there's welcoming
in such a courtesy; not merely exorcise:
I'd like to talk at this late stage on equal terms,
declare a kind of coming of age
to those who have implanted death in me.

And yet I'm only staring into empty drawers
and cupboards where a sediment of dust has dropped
on papers with dead dates and on events
in a world that looks naïver than my own.

The streets drag down to docks – to warehouses,
derricks, pigeons, and hard men
that I resisted twenty years ago
by riding inland, choosing softer options
they would say.

                    I think perhaps
it's time to gauge whatever love
there was or might have been, or time
to ask the dead to let me estimate
their suffering by the yardstick of my flesh,
time at last to come home to myself.

Once

Never gave death
much thought those days:
the dead were too illustrious
to be brooded on, too
well spoken of, so much
part of the brickwork.

Different now: the dead
are too expensively alive
in the bone, the membrane,
the organ out of tune,
as to suggest parents,
unbidden, come ghosting back
to set examples after all.

Only Child

Big-headed from the start,
my soft skull's flowering
judged neither beautiful
nor blessable –

                    a clenched,
a brute fist bearing down.

Did I do that? – stretch their love
to screaming. So that he

would never put her through
that kind of thing again.

Home

A sunset's bloodying the sky outside.
The embankment's black. She is making up
his carrying-out, corned beef, boiled eggs.
I lie awake above the kitchen taps,
my ears on fire. I've listened to
dragged furniture, smashed plates;
I've heard him spit my name at her.

I count the stairs, squat down upon
the thirteenth one. His oilskin stinks
of creosote, hangs, black bat,
above me on a hook. I need to measure honesty.
Will he keep his word
to send me *packing to a Home...ears
pinned back...bread and dripping once a day*?

After Such Knowledge
(for Geoffrey Holloway on his 70th birthday)

He unbuckled and the buckle-end
of his swung belt floored me,
pants down, and getting my what-for.

And what for too?
I the back of the air raid shelter ·
had simply unbuckled; my belt
was worm-clasped and Shirl-
from-two-doors-down had eyed the worm
and dropped her navy-blues
to show what-for-eventually.

So I was what?
right for a belt at seven years.

That washday Monday his longjohns
were battering the air that I
rummaging for grown-up things
in Shirley's drawers was sinning in.

What undid me? Mother
prying into cock-eyed flies
unbuttoning me for bed.

Studio Portrait

My sepia great-grandmother
stares out from time
before my time – a time
ingenuous with flowers
and solid parlour furniture,
spindle-legged, high-backed,
as if someone's
just wheeled her in to do
an Old Ma Riley party piece
she will decline uncertainly.

To think of fear so decorous,
so buttoned up. Her only flesh
is head and hands
and head is level with those flowers
a dicky-birding man intends
as obvious analogy.
At her throat
like a trained beetle squats
a cameo brooch. And hands
display with rings
connections and fidelities.
And eyes are swift and vivid with
disasters – splintering rope,
the plunging down through holds,
the barely understood
gunning down in No Man's Land.

This face I could have kissed.
Not that wax
my mother held me up to see
in a room
they'd blinded out the daylight from
in a time
that had already started to
be mine. And death's.

Confirmation

He screwed it together
winking at me as much as to say
we don't let everybody know.

I was handing him bits of crozier,
silver bits – and was the other
ebony? – from a case
much like a musical instrument's
in the billowing vestry.

It was my Confirmation Day.

But this was more confirming
than his hands laid on
my brylcreemed and immaculate quiff
in front of mother and tense aunts.

I looked to wink at him but he
was mitre'd and professional.

There was starch in my surplice
and my leader's medal, brasso'd, glowed.

Family

Some nights, late,
he wobbled home from work
in oilskins streaming rain,
his soaked cap limp,
on a bike that bounced
the dockyard cobbles,
                              bevvied up
and in the mood
for striking out
at all the grim estrangements
in his life:
                  an ulcer
brought home with his conscience
from the war which banished him
from ships that steamed beyond
the river mouth, dragging smoke
below the fixed horizon
into other worlds;
                              a wife
whose proper pieties
would only yield to sentiments
coaxed out of him which he,
before and afterwards, despised;
                                        and me
the son she knitted with a vengeance for.

And yet at weekends
we were Family. Keen-eyed streets
confirmed him Master when
he led us out to cinemas
or relatives – a dandy
double-breasted man,
raffish in trilby like George Raft,
he looked
that cut-above-the-rest
they knew his wife to be
but puzzled over in the son
who wore a treachery,
the impudence of knowledge in his eyes.

Class Photograph
(for Willie Wardle)

In the loft a cardboard box
of overshuffled memories
and collapsed-in histories,
                                there,
somewhere among the innocent
I knew I'd find us out.

You're bottom right, cross-legged,
uncertain with your hands,
your smile; and I'm top left,
cub-badged, hair parted wrong,
precarious five rows up.

You'd think to look at us
a chord has just been bashed
upon the upright, Miss
Bingham barbirolli-ing and
OneTwoThree 'Ye Banks and Braes'!

or sirens any second now
will scramble all the lads across
the gritty Gray Street yard
to revving Lancasters, the girls
yelling in the slipstreams
waving off.

                That's Swiftie
in the wellies; there's John Wilson,
Eddie Williams, Alan Coutts; that's
Philip Gardner next to me,
Professor now; and Reggie Bennett
dead.
                Why can't I name a single girl?

It's forty years of shuffling,
collapsing cards. Your hand still bears
Miss Bingham's straightnesses:
you write of Unemployment in
an Overspill.

I climbed the ladder
to the loft and turned up this:
scuffed knees, Bowles Street dewdrop,
forward-looking eyes.

Miss Bingham

It's Miss Bingham's sense
they must come round to
when whisky makes
the letters fall about.

It's her sit-up-straight
they must obey,
Janet-and-John
uprightness taught

in characters that she
made blackboard-bold
to toil us with
in Standard Two.

Everything I write
remembers her,
has her hand in it
and falls short.

Mrs Clancy

wasn't tense and willowy
fussing the Nature Table's twigs
like tall Miss Fairclough,

nor tweedy-posh like kind
Miss Bingham with her
copperplate and poetry,

nor young and rashly lipsticked
like pretty Miss Taylor
biking homewards over cobbles
to toughen up her tennis thighs:

she was hard as ground
ice grabs hold of;

used the streets' snide
and whinge against us,
mimicked mother's tongue
or father's fist,

made small hands scat
like rabbits over desks,

rapped knuckles with
the rat-bite of
her twelve-inch rule.

Complicity
for Philip Gardner...

who wound the hire car window down
and offered acid drops – sugar-grained
to rasp the tongue, a sour sweet
from dusty corner shops and cobbled streets,
our grey diurnal trudge to school's
black workhouse brick some forty years
ago. Is this how old our friendship is:
from my First Morning with cacked kecks,
a scalding pus down backs of legs
in Akie Street, to this once-more
departure, you flown in from Newfoundland
researching yet another book? your bag
of sweets a direct line from serge
short pants to glove compartment
gesturing doggedly across oceans
and the years of our complicity
in one another's altered, altering lives.

You were a bus in Gray Street School,
whizzed playgrounds like a lunatic,
screeched halts, climbed out to change
indicators, all the stops of Merseyside
and Lancashire, going everywhere intensely,
brum-brumming through the gears.

Now you're in gear again. After a whiskied night
of swapping poems, did we catch in one another's eyes,
shyly, almost like lovers once betrayed
but long-ago forgiven, something more profound
than farewell, adieu, goodbye-till-next...
recognising the one goodbye that must come
as absolute, a first rehearsal of an end
to all that's tenuous and precious, forty years
of sweet-sour slowly rolling on the tongue.

To Tom in Canada

His skin was bruised like windfall fruit,
bronchitis rattled at his throat. I should
have written then – discovering him, your father,
destitute like that; but shock's a thing
the heart will hoard.

                    The visit was
disguised, a casual calling-in, our
annual fixture of surprise. No longer
belonging, we looked official, parked
in the old-rope grey of that cold street.

Where there'd be
warm welcoming again I steered
my daughter to a house I'd once
learnt love in, for her to attest to certainties
that congregate along the years,
                              expecting him
not much more altered than that owlish clock
which sanctioned all the house contained.

The clock still swings its pendulum.
But he is dead; and you,
leaping the Atlantic to a father's grave
that neatly, quickly closed on him,
have come and gone.

In one short afternoon we blankly stared
together at the estuary, across the beach
with all its mob of ghostly gulls, where once
we'd towed daft girls and swivelled foot-
marks in damp sand, sceptically interpreting
our fathers' war, watching their concrete pyramids
sink, emplacements fill with sand and flies.
Then back to streets with poets' names
which now fall to another blitz.

                              We are
an age when deaths begin to tell on us,
queueing up to test our nerve. Love does this
to all of us. As we walked the Esplanade,
did you feel it sharpening?

An Adenoidal Letter to a Former Classmate

*'Liverpudlian' plays self-mockingly on the idea of 'pool'. I
was born in Liverpool. I would be flattering myself if I claimed
that you need to be a comedian to survive there. But Liver-
pudlians do, like punsters, switch things about: they breathe
through their mouths and talk through their noses. They are
physiological, existential twisters.*

WALTER REDFERN: Puns

It always was a question of getting on
in life, in years. A long way now
from our mothers' simple tontine dreams
of being free of factories, corner shops,
uncouth docks and home's accumulating
bitternesses; a long way too
from fathers' hopeless optimisms,
their grimacings at love or luck.
                              The docks
are emptying. Here's one drained,
a good-for-nothing siltscape glistening;
and here's another shop blanked out,
a warehouse where a masochistic wind
cuts itself to pieces on smashed panes.

What's left is just another place
for dying in...queasy bedrooms and
inhospitable wards. One has to laugh.

E Pluribus Unum

Reggie Bennett? wonk-eyed, awkward,
a pustuled butt
squirming in conscience all these years...

'Pluribus mensibus,' said text and teacher
and Wonk-Eyed Awkward next to me, stumped,
was whimpering Help!

Free to squawk, seagulls perched
on prefab classrooms and the town
was full of trams. I whispered wickedly

'mensibus? that's *mensa*, table!' God forgive.
It was a trick he triumphed with:
'The boy,' he braved, 'came home from school

having learnt many tables!' – cute enough
to have him thumped and me the one
pluribus years afterwards who squirms

for a dadless Bunter-boy in clinic specs
('down there in London...long-haired...
forehead tattoo'd like an Indian') dead.

Latin Master

Thou didst betray me to a lingring book,
And wrap me in a gown.

With detentions, impositions, cuffs,
he practised his imperial rule
on 'idlers', occupying minds
with legions of the strictest words
footslogged into Liverpool
on a bellyful of ancient deaths.

He altered all our history,
until the sea
seemed to lose its dragging power
and we learnt to hate our dockland streets
and know ourselves barbarian.

His Latin verbs put me to work
inside the fort,
made turncoat of me in the end.

Even his kindness after four o'clock
when he cranked a wind-up gramophone
inviting in his blue-eyed boys
to share the spoils
of Bach cantatas, symphonies by Brahms,
lost us our purchase on the things of home,
made traitors of us to our kind.

Joe Ellis, English Teacher

In a scrag-end classroom, jerry-built
after the War, Joe Ellis chalked
the dirty bits from Shakespeare up
while lorries trundled to drab docks
down Balliol Road. We learnt to grin
the other side of poetry.
                              A man
no one dared bowdlerise, he taught us
drunk, chain-smoked, and swore:
our respectable headmaster was
'that Belgian bastard', popinjay
and martinet; and looking Meanings up
(like 'popinjay' and 'martinet')
meant taking out our 'big red dics'.

He gave us poetry
like giving away his last half-crown
because it was good to give away.

After his death
some words shook loose:
we heard of years of broken marriage,
of the son she'd kept away from him,
how cancer scorched his body in the end.
It helped to explain his mischief,
his grip on words he loved,
his grip on love itself.

COLLECTING BEETLES
Bootle to Cambridge, 1955-58
(for George Szirtes)

The past, which remains forever another place.

But it does spill over. It is what we are
And what we see and time and again forget.
GEORGE SZIRTES

No pursuit at Cambridge was followed with
nearly so much eagerness or gave me so much
pleasure as collecting beetles.
CHARLES DARWIN

A Picture Palace View of a Liverpool Headmaster

Responsible for sending me up, me a Bootle scruff,
up to genteel Cambridge, this dapper man
modelling himself on night club movie stars,
tuxedoed toffs who fooled around with Garbo,
sipped highballs with Lana Turner and by the end
inherited million dollar corporations
from blustering uncles with cigars then settled down
with pert stenographers or goldenhearted hatcheck girls.

I always expected the comic part – tap-dancing, crooning,
the chirpy junior taken on from hardluck streets
to skivvy in basements, stock up shelves, in search
of a break, hoping to catch the boss's eye,
step out towards that something big – a seat on the Board,
my own convertible with whitewalled tyres, a set-the-date
with a glamour-puss daughter of the chief:

questions of degree and class.

University Challenge

Did a bunk, became a monk: buck-toothed, horn-rimmed,
that goofy teacher who in Bootle said,
'Serious about Literature? Then read this!'
plonking a heavyweight and off-the-syllabus
Tom Jones down on the desk. What was the test?
The page barrier? Unending scurrying print?
Sixth-form overseriousness, literary long-face?
Or was it virginity he was anxious for: blind date
with Henry Fielding masterfully pimped?

Prior to Going Up

I sweat six weeks in Robinson's Foundry in Bowles Street
baking cores till they resemble shrunken charred Swiss rolls,
packing moulds with finest sand, casting esoteric chunks
of ships. It's not just 'student' that gets up their nose
but 'Cambridge'; and it's no use telling where I live,
over there in Bulwer Street, under the embankment, or that
my dad's a rigger, comes home pissed. 'We know your sort,
ploughing through the shite of all them fucking dons,' they say,
and 'Here y-are, petal, back up on to this!' – cruel solidarity
of muscle, ignorance, files scraping away at vices, white-
hot crucibles, all setting questions I'm prepared to fail, that is
until, ordered to 'take one end' by that bastard foreman they all hate,
I pour neon-white metal down the throats of moulds
and accidentally ('accidentally on purpose' they all cheer)
spill the hot honey over his stupid frigging bigot boot.

Landlady
(for Gordon)

It suited, the three years there
in sight of clanky sidings, timber yards,
mnemonic of grandparental 'home' that kept
us off-the-peg scholars jokily in place;
chastened too, with its one-step-back into
a widow world of jug-and-basin early light,
outside-loo in shivering rain,
and deadly dentured Chapel grin
hovering over breakfast
brittle with bacon, charred fried bread.

A blurred world even then – the colours dried
out of wallpapers, furniture in dingy rooms
that smelt of the departed; remember that
ashy embered gloaming where she rocked,
deaf almost as death, under the unwarlike eyes
of a Tommy Atkins brother dead at Ypres,
tortoise shell frames of improbable husband
and only son – those histories, that love
we could hardly credit, never quite construct.

We were her 'gentlemen'
with back-homes she believed were strict
and honourable, 'sports' whose earnest games
were played with books in lofty halls
of ancient privilege – and in fact
thinking ourselves gatecrashers, with Scouse
accents rubbed smooth by radio, with bummed
orange-box shelves that housed a clutch
of secondhand opinions, our LPs of rasped-silk
Julie London, velvet Ella, torrid Peggy Lee.

It seems improbable, all so long ago – with her
long shunted out of this disinheriting world.

Conscience on Mill Road

Blinking into daylight,
brazening it out, coming back
past stern East Anglian faces
and shops, all afternoon
despite me, getting on:

back from a hot hour's wallow
at the Public Baths
or the pear-drop darkness of
a matinee of laconic Bogeys,
pouting Bardots, Eastmancolor
canyons, sulky James Deans,
back to the smell of austerity,
the must of all those books.

Album

I *Photographing the First Years*

Tableau: catlicked chaps on grey Museum lawns
in gowns grinning for lenses; the Master's just
delivered his vision-of-the-good-life chat;
the Museum is solidly behind them and autumn's
shuffling leaves in the different-feeling air.
Sightseers in the portico are sanctioning
the fleetingness of this, as if just being there
they print themselves on history too.

II *Fresher*

This one in Trinity under the famous sundial
where I'm mock-curtseying in brandnew gown
– not to put too fine a point on it – represents
in 1955 a kind of ragged-trousered muscling-in
on history, a comic apprehension of having just as much
right being there as anyone: a bright uncomplicated face
keen for the contest of subversions coming up...

Museum Pieces

Leavis astride a warhorse of a bike
quixotic in Trumpington Street, his tanned
and freckled bonce a badly-varnished egg,
the flaunted open-neck that I mistook
for Working Class Sympathy giving the look,
the unmistakable sneer of an unkempt Byron.

And biking matronly on King's Parade,
Sylvia, her basket bubbling apples
greenly, heading for Grantchester Meadows
where Granta glides and larks ascend
warningly, heading for Heathcliff, love.

C.S. Lewis guest-lecturing on Courtly Love,
the lion-look of Aslan in Mill Lane;
and Empson once, dervish whiskers' orange fire
blasting us to outer space with Donne.

Elizabeth Zeeman's slide show
of Brueghel's 'vigorous' peasants she
peopled Chaucer with, while we with wanhope
watched her litel breathings lift her breasts.

And Dadie, Noel in mortar-boards near Senate House
nostrilled like thoroughbreds and in charge of
everything: purple/yellow crocuses along
the Backs, Forster's welfare tucked away in King's,
the Ceremonies of Carols, flow-rate of the Cam,
willows, madrigals, May Balls
                              and yours truly,
feet tapping to Shakespearean rags
(Tillyard, Muir and Wilson Knight) and like
a jazz club junkie fidgety for the real
fix of the Goon Show Tuesday half-past eight;

but mostly you, old Rembrandt, got up
like a foolish weary warrior in the Fitzwilliam Museum,
wheeled out to play charades and wisely keeping up
the old guessing game.

Up Till Then

In my case too Larkin's right
about sex rearing a sixties' head.
Full sex that is. Not just back-
row gooeyness in the dark
of Carltons, Gainsboroughs
with technicolor cowboys
banging away and hired dicks
in clinches with Bacall,
Ruth Roman, Myrna Loy:

always avoiding films
that irritated laughter,
huge asthmatic oooooooohs of hers
too orgasmic publicly.
                  That was
as much as we knew then
and thought might be enough
until the dare of Continental films:
Dangerous Woman, Wedding Night,
Bardot in wet t-shirts,
the pissoirs of Clochemerle.

The Beatles? Not yet for us.
In any case, I went to the Cavern
Thursday nights and twisted to –
what was her name? –
the cool of complicated jazz.

Dating

I *Keeping in Touch*

A long impressive road from Bootle-where-the-bugs-wear-clogs
to dazzling Cambridge; and really, Viv, you were better off
held back by begging letters, brittle rhymes, better kept
for homecomings, touching scenes at the foot of the stairs,
or at goodnight gates in a trance of Woolies' scent, or in
the public dark of cinemas where we measured inches of
retreat/advance as if we measured miles and years. Believe me,
I'm grateful for all those hot bewilderments which I lugged back
each new term with the incomprehensions my poor parents had
wrung from me for proudly disappointing them – your hand
sometimes noncommittal, limp, mouth brutally thin.

II *Head Over Heels*

Who was that other I weekended in London with,
the one I ended swapping for her friend? the one
each time I took her out you'd guarantee would trip
and fall – pavements, plush theatre stairs, the path
beside the Serpentine, down jazz club steps –
Margaret someone, middle-class and dumb, who fell
for 'Cambridge' and for naïve student me
who, thirty years ago and more, fell briefly too
for – inverted commas! – 'London', 'middle class'.

III *Part of History*

That skinny girl from Lewisham, met in postcard Spain
(above a panting bay, Glenn Miller music smooched):
because of her I grin an old photograph astride
a splintery burro, flaunt a cheap sombrero, show a sun-
tanned thigh; because of her in an old diary I record
seeing Khrushchev and Bulganin drive a London street
and Khrushchev looked me in the eye and waved; because
of her I've kept this old matt snap in which, eyes closed,
she leans against a tree, all vague with time
and camera shake – a corny fifties Bardot pose –
the pout and all – somewhere along the Cambridge Backs.

IV *And Then Angela*

Crossing Atlantics on havana cigars: Papa –
proper blockerman, captain for Cunard, and not
a bad old stick – got up to shake my hand;
and Mummy – a Hat at Morning Services, who had
attended Garden Parties and knew the form,
absolute I had no chance; and Angela –
O Angela, you were beautiful, the very goods!
Mona Lisa English rose: I could genuinely
foolishly have married you (except you loved
Sinatra and shopping in George Henry Lee's
too much); could easily have settled down with you
and ours, pastorally in a Cheshire somewhere,
and be writing my nth successful sneaky book
about what people do (depressions, infidelities)
in mock-tudor double-garage leafy avenues.
It was, I remember, your Twenty-First
and Mummy was just having to point out
him over there…from the richest Wirral family…
how everybody thought that you and he…
O Angela, I truly loved you for that while: I asked
what number of cows there'd be for dowry.
I was never really sure of you – perhaps you were
too lazy to give me up just yet; I can't
now recall what happened to 'us' – but Mummy
must have smirked when you mentioned it.

Vacation Jobs

Two summers a shipwrights' labourer
my Old Man wangled, of me humping
toolbags, timber, learning to batten
hatches, tom-off cars down holds;
then a single summer in the General Stores
among old men like budgies chunnering
in dingy corners of quayside sheds...

same Company he was foreman rigger for,
same grey gull-infested wharves
and yellow-funnel boats that slogged
the South America run: his world
and workplace where he knew respect...

ask anyone, Old Lars, Pongo, Billy Molloy,
ask any skipper, engineer, or mate along
the line of docks: always a good word,
a tot or two, a backhander bottle of
Bacardi rum for him...

who bungled things back home,
across the nervous tablecloth or in
the blue flicker of telly or loud behind
bedroom doors: he wanted me to witness
the respect he walked about in there,
along wharves, over decks, in messrooms,
to know what I was forfeiting, know it for real.

Local

The accent back home —
The more you hide it
The broader it gets.

JAPANESE SENRYŪ (trs. Bownas & Thwaite)

I want him to believe that there's no difference, side,
    (there has never been congruity),
that I can stand my round, can hold my ale
    (I cannot hold my ale),
one cocksure elbow on the bar, feeling at home
    (I'll never feel at home again),
one foot up on the rail, and knocking back pints
    (can never be the best)
along with the best. 'My lad,' he introduces,
    (good at being "genuine"),
'he's at Cambridge University.' He knows
    (knows his own bullshit too)
my interest's academic when I talk to him
    (however I try to talk to him)
of boxers, jockeys, or just the price
    (cuanta costa? he will ask)
of shirts or shoes I've bought in town
    (congratulates a bargain every time).
'When is it then you're going back?' he says
    (wants the place without me, mother to himself)
'Tomorrow,' I say, 'ten-thirty. Like the same again?'
    (perhaps his favourite rum and pep?)

After the May Ball Is Over

In El Patio, pronounced Payshee-o,
in Sydney Street, sucking through
the in-thing froth of espresso coffee-o,

a steamed-up cross between dishwater and
Ovaltine – and cubicled in pine,
sauna-fresh, *contemporary*, planned –

hither the Heroes and the Nymphs resort,
the champers lot, the hunt-ball broads,
to sip from pyrex beakers, brag of sport.

Here's one this morning's quite whey-faced:
'You slept with Betty then last night?
Oh shocking bad taste!'

Punts are back from Grantchester,
couchez-vous Madame?
Like dead gudgeon condoms fester
along the nauseous Cam.

A Day Randomly Picked from the Diary 1956

Supervision, John for coffee,
squash, Nabil 3pm, Nabil's for tea,
Phil and John round for the Goons.

An essay on Shakespeare's Last Plays
toeing the Tillyard line about Renewal,
Redemptions, drudged that weekend
in Devonshire Road's greyness, the fug
of Erinmore Flake, and boldly read out to
a shy wobbly man in College (Big Fat Ron)
who droned embarrassed comment and doled out
another title for next week 'something on
the Gothic Novel...suggest you read...'

And coffee where? what talked about?
his strictures on our essays, John?
his double chins, the sea-lion look
of sadness and uncertainty, what he meant
by Orthodox Assumptions in the plays?

I remember dropping squash as too
competitive; but I've no idea about Nabil,
unless he was that sternly sloppy chap,
that Evangelical with missionary naivety
and crumpets, saving souls for Billy Graham's sake.

Evening half-past eight: Philip,
oldest friend (still) and John, the newest
(no longer), convulsive with Ying Tong:
scholars from the blitzkrieg and liberated Europe,
brains from bombed sites, eyes watery
with disbelieving joy.

Establishment

Disingenuous in Woolworths
asking the price
of *Wet Paint* and directed to
'that other counter, over there!'
by fenland mardiness;

and swearing in Catalan
with poor Federico apoplectic,
hissing *Hush* like a cheek-
busting cherub in a map:
four thousand times balls,
I shit in the sea!

       Remember
two far-back hearties there?
satirical, loud: 'I say old man
I never knew the likes of you
frequented this august
establishment!'

       I wanted
to smack him in his fat
gob-full-of-plums and might have done
had I not suddenly felt
a perverse and velvety itch
working at my fingertips, a memory
of red baize, a rustle of
semi-transparent envelopes,
gaudy exotic foreign stamps,
once in Bootle Woolies, Stanley Road,
a smart-alec grammar boy filching.

Invitation to Join

A poem accepted for *Delta* began it all,
the one about Pam Adamson,
our vicar's eldest girl who went
to a posh school in Crosby, and me
gazing up at her window
imagining she brushed her hair,
dogging her steps to bus stops
when she sailed off to satisfy
lascivious dates and treacheries at
the tennis club.

               'You must come round
to Levenson's in Downing!' Wasn't that
where Leavis ruled the literary roost?
I took my BBC'd Scouse accent and intoned
'Here's one about a fairground in the rain.
The setting is a park in Bootle...'
Faces strained interest, to hear
the aderoidal verse. Then someone said,
'Good word, that "polyglot" – but how
does it apply to soggy booths?'

Stammering to a glass of reddish plonk
I heard myself:
'No idea. Just liked the bloody sound of it.'

Posing Near St Johns

I

This lad in the baggy duffel coat
            his dad
has "borrowed" from a First Mate on a liner
            lounging
at berth in Liverpool points a pipe stem
            dashingly at
some daft idea of future near the Bridge
            of Sighs.
The coat he wears has swaggered up
            companionways
in tilting seas, outfaced Atlantic gales,
            seen icebergs,
strolled dangerous quaysides in New York.
            The A-levelled lad
is studying English Literature, has just
            discovered
Salinger's breakdowns when you flunk.

II

No one's going to point at *them*,
catch them out as common, loud,
            especially
            no camera:
this handsome couple from where d'you say?
            from Liverpool.

His drycleaned overcoat hangs just right,
tie is sober, knot a gem
            of neatness;
            hair is
catlicked down, his buffed-up brogues
            shining.

She too is looking good: brandnew coat,
Christmas diamante brooch from him
                    glamorously
                    angled;
new shoes, new gloves, with matching bag
                    from Lewis's.

His mam and dad! This for them is holiday,
swans and willows on the Backs:
                    they want him
                    to be
proud of them, not be ashamed among his
                    brainy mates.

He's steered them tactfully here
through a maze of courtyards,
                    past chapels,
                    weighty statues,
to pose them for posterity beneath
                    immemorial trees.

      III

On the poop and upright,
now with the knack of punting,
pole-end gripping gravel,

on course and steady,
steady as she goes: fancies himself
Roundhead, pikestaff thrust at smugness,

ruffling mallard, scurrying roach,
smashing reflections,
bringing down battlements

for the hell of it; and watching as,
possessively, dispassionately,
it all re-forms behind.

Hi Fi
(for J.E.A.)

Your kind of poetry I supposed:
wired up to tweeters, woofers,
tuned in to the mousiest vibrations,
twitchiest feedback, frequencies
no one else could catch.
                          I
was plugged in to metaphor,
languishing in tricksy rhyme,
posting sarky Audenesques
to hopeless girls back home.

Do you remember your Leicester
fiancée up one weekend, hair
yanked tightly back to honour
Fonteyn; how from a faded rug
before an honest gasfire she let
music lift her suddenly
like some afraid wild thing?
I think I thought of Ibsen:
'Why Nora dear, you dance as if
it were a matter of your life!'

That day of departures, '58,
with its long-since-lapsed
professions of faith and frequency,
I watched you brush the static out
of Elgar; that day *Nimrod* became
the test of all fidelities.

Calling Up Over Christmas
(for Geoff)

Better off than Bootle me: Liverpool College
(where they paid), a bit of a bursary
(your old man's bank), house tucked away
in shrubbery out West Derby way.

Not so posh as to be without
Scouse quick wit, deflating mockeries,
relish for things ludicrous, the simply daft.
We clever dicks joined forces,

found common language for
our Cambridge adventure: a mix
of Itma, Goon Show, Lime Street, which
so intensified the dialect of the tribe

they thought we came from Africa!
Remember that loof (that backward fool)
once in the Junior Common Room (we'd not
long finished our braised pigeon

flunky-served among oak panelling
and smirky portraits of the dead): a loud
hee-haw accent, very best Down-South,
that found us 'jolly interesting, by Jove!'

And that Festival of Classic Westerns at the Arts
culminating in *Shane* and you protesting
(sucked-in-suddenly oh-how-dare-you breaths!)
'No proper Cowie! There was no singin' in it, la!'

Now a once-a-Christmas call – you in Cambridge, me
suburban Liverpool, and lecturers both – to check
over our Famous Collections of Hinges (swap that one
off the Kaiser's iron leg for one off the old Ark Royal?)
and wish each other junket by the bucketful again.

The Death Has Occurred...

...of Ralph Vaughan Williams. Sad August 1958:
my Cambridge is over; and now, more loved
than either grandfather, this man I count on for
my deeper self, is dead. I sit on a Liverpool
Corporation bus, jolting its dull green way towards
the docks, towards my in-between-things job
with iron ships, hugging a neurotic degree and this,
today's bleak news, past black warehouses, cranes,
listening to elegies inside my head: across
a dozen counties a single violin's exquisite grief.

*   *   *

The Last Days of Pompeii

'The story of explosive human passions in the
shadow of an awakening volcano...391 pages.'

I ought to read it, having been
brought up in Bulwer Street.

Edward Lytton Bulwer, afterwards
Lord Lytton (1803-73), that
'hummiest of bugs' – the Book Club
can't know that he,
in my father's gross codologies,
my boyhood's weekend dandyism
of gaudy tie and cultured quiff,
is family too.

I ought to show more loyalty.

And there's another link to make
this dusty grammar of disaster mine:
flattened, burnt by bombs, our street
has claims on dignity. I too
heard rumblings in the night.

Now after all these years of poetry
I sit with books in Boundary Drive,
weighing up Sir Walter Scott's cold words
on Bulwer's 'slang tone of morality'
and Queenie's labelling him the first
of modern best-sellers.

Remembering too
how in his final landlocked weeks
my dying father asked
for 'reading books' and I had said
I'd nothing that he'd like.

Bootle Streets

Salt winds keep these ocean-minded streets
voyaging. There are men here who, landlubbered
(wedded, winded, ulcered out), still walk as if
steel decks were rolling underfoot: riggers
and donkeymen, dockhands and chandlers,
shipwrights and scalers, who service ships
with something of love's habits, insisting on
manhood and sweet memories.

Look in one bedroom. On
the glass-topped dressing table stood
a carved war-painted coconut Aztec head –
to me, memento mori, shrunken thing,
who watched death dredge this bed.
And yet for years it was a trophy,
souvenir of all the thousand miles
of furrowed brine, of fragrant isles.
Consider my mother's photograph beside,
her scissored form revealed against
a satin ground of South American butterflies,
wings of phosphorescent blue,
of tropic midnight, bluer than any sky
that ever settled round these roofs.

My father's second, widowed wife
lies in that bed remembering
holidays in Spain, while I
the other end of the city build,
from images of boyhood, paper boats.

Homecoming

Due on the tide, my father's rusted hulk,
weary from landings at Sicily, sailed
into blitzed Liverpool under the waving swords
of searchlights, into the flash and batter of
the ack-ack guns. Under a sky in panic,
into the erupting port, up-river he came
urging home his helpless and unspeaking love.

Next morning, docked, he slung his canvas bag
about his shoulders like a drunken mate, himself
unsteady in the smoking, settling air, and walked
into our street, turning the corner by
the foundry. The street was flattened – brick and wood
in scorched disorder. 'I thought that you were goners,'
he afterwards said, finding us safe up-town
at my grandma's house.

And I remember the last few days,
the quivering run-up hours to that street's death:
a five-year-old and his mother hunched
under the stairs, with the fat chrome springs
of an obsolete pram jigging over my head
and plaster puffing white dust in our hair,
the sky droning and tingling blasts
as a neighbouring street went down.

'We moved that day,' my mother used to say,
'and that same night your dad came home.'
She prized the weird coincidence. It was
as if someone had given her flowers.

Whatsit & Whoever

Halfway down the prefab'd street
a polished car. Wednesday.
Her fancyman giving Mrs Whatsit one
under rattling cranes.

And a storming night in Akie Street
and another, high-heeled, screeching
'That way t' yer ship when y' come out!'

And Sven, Lars, or Whoever hearing nothing,
not even the wind's hostilities.
Nothing happened except
a swaying, a staggering, a dance
his body could no longer understand.

'Now don't you forget!' she yelled

to shame the streets' hypocrisies.

Peer Group

A saga world. Legal wrangles in the street,
dust-bin shields, split heads,
bonfire raids and debris feuds.

Darkness fell on it. A final dusk
gathering us to ordered homes.

Except our leaders. They were cursed
to live the hard-knock legend out.

Wife-beaters, wrestlers, drunkards, thieves,
they kept the rules, maintained the style,
in spite of blackboards, rulers, canes.

As big as lorries, five proud sons
who took the road their father took,

boxed, joined the parachute brigade,
stole crates of whisky from the docks,
did time, and kept my boyhood whole
as something I betrayed
by growing out of, sailing out of sight.

Bonfire Night and Mr Ellison

On the bombed side of the street,
before they plonked those shoe-box prefabs down,
we raised our bonfire, roofing it
with planks we'd nicked from Barney's Yard.
And when night came and we were still
awake in all its wickedness,
we prodded rolled newspaper torches in
between the planks to let the fire rip.

But in the awe of it, the hush,
we heard the Elloes' drunken father curse
and clatter like a one-man-band
along the street. And next,
the pistol shot of a slammed front door,
his whingeing wife,
thin as a needle, quick as a pain,
dragging off four yapping dogs of sons
around the foundry corner
and away up Knowsley Road.

No one called me in. I was left
with a bonfire playing merry hell
with the dark, while half-seas Mr Ellison,
tottering like a bull come round
from surgery, hauled out and flung
curtains, chairs, and table legs
among the splintering flames. And moved
by generosity: 'There's something
for your bommy, Matt.'

Finally the sideboard's bulk.
But halfway across the cobbled street
strength and fury failed. 'I'll have
a bloody bommy by meself,' he said,
striking matches into drawers.

Just two of us, alone, with darkness winning:
me not twelve years old, and him
slumped on the kerbstones, blubbering.

Old Ma Lennon

praised the Lord for Guinness
and people who were good-as-gold.
And all the lines about her face I swore
were never age's but laughter's
perfecting of itself. Perhaps our Bootle
dockland streets conspired to keep
her peasant innocence intact
so someone from them might at least
get into Heaven by a smile.

Now villains, sulky no-goods have the house
that once smelt faintly rancid like an old
and shabby sacristy, where once
her lacquered saints, that watercolour Jesus
tendering simple and exacting love,
were honoured.

If only for her, I would protest
the existence of her Heaven, an eternity
of laughter, smiles; a perpetuity of stout.

Nextdoor's Garden

In summer, grasses
tall and tough as wheat.
She was too old and he, her nephew,
was too dim
for the kind of order gardens need
to look their Sunday Best.

We used to blame our weeds on them:
dandelions, docks,
nudging with peasant clumsiness
our pinks and marigolds aside.
It was sectarian, a rivalry
of roots. We knew she kept
their dingy rooms
plain at saints' behests
to keep a faith with martyrdoms.

Those grasses aimed their seeds
at where our orange lilies grew;
their thistles landed on our lawns,
lodged in the seams of paving stones
my father laid. And efforts
of tidiness, our symmetries,
now faded into tolerance
as I have grown through deaths,
were mocked by their wild garden's
over-populating seed.

And that corridor of trodden path
that went beneath her washing line
was via dolorosa,
where she amid the alien grass
was Mater Mysteria attending
the depositions of shirts.

Getting the World Right

'Aye, once we get
a Protestant Pope!'
my father cheeked
shawlies in the snug,
hard-nosed chars
clattering gangplanks
and early-morning mops.

Nextdoor's would
have scowled. Across
a creosoted fence
we scarcely spoke,
their lad-my-age
and me. Sometimes
at the coal-shed
and him at the bin,
scraping cinders,
shovelling coal,
I'd try 'Too cold
for this...'

He could expect
at worst his dad's
I-Thought-I-Told,
at best a few
Hail-Marys-worth.
I was earnest, I
was righting history, I
was challenging wrongs.

Something Electrical
his dad – tricky
fingers: wasn't he
the first tinkerer
(dropping spanners,
dripping oil) along
our street. And my
old man – wasn't he,
with his grubby bike,

just one of daft
King Billy's Lads,
planting lilies,
backgarden marigolds,
outrageous orange
joke-shop bombs.

And Bootle to You

Two hundred miles
deeper into diffidence:

in the wind a brutal town,
slate roofs, pinched streets.

Going north, our wedding day,
the worst winter in years.

You never understood the joke:
('This, mam, dad, is Monika!')
'Can't wait to see their face,'
I said.

        You shivered
in the back bedroom I
was awkward in for twenty years:

embankments, warehouses,
familiar sky
clawed at by cranes.

In the kitchen under us,
was that laughter, the joke on us,

bringing more than we bargained for,
more than ourselves?

Calling on the Off Chance

Still unused to cars
the kerb I'm parked at
thinks I'm here about
a burglary, a policy,
bad debt. My old street
eyes me as, importantly,
suspiciously, I strain
against glare to peer
through windows, probe
the letter box,
glimpse stairs,
the lino where ('had hoped
to catch you in')
my scribble lands.

I kid myself. The street's
clueless, knows nothing.
Television's sucked
everything dry.

       Still
half in love with dead
film star faces – mother's
Merle Oberon and father's
gangsterish good looks,
I'm playing gumshoe,
getting colder on the scent
of innocence,
that black-and-white morality
that kept us dazzled
in the dark.

       She's out,
my stepmother – at shops
or at a sister's plusher house.
The foundry on the corner's now
a Car Repair Shop crudely spelt
in patchwork gloss. Outside,
oily overalls debate
a Ford's contrariness,
heads deep in trouble
nothing to do with me.

The Ghost of My Mother

What of her history when all the traces
are of him: his hairs bunched in the nose,
the excremental wax that clogs my ears,
a moody sea at work in the veins?
Her death alone was memorable,
a blood-burst in the mouth.
She was his victim – much as I
still carting round his blustering ghost
that beat her down. What of her
when I revamp his tantrums
and sudden shamefaced tenderness
that buys back love with promises,
embittered dreams of something good?
Ghosts are rarely charitable.
And now she nudges me,
with frightened, loving eyes.

Rigger's Wife

Winter, always mean
on love, came in
from wind-possessed black wharves,
its muscles tensed
like hawsers taut with ice.
She learnt to expect
its bullying,
to cope, to count
its pennies wrenched
from days as stiff as slate,
fingering them until they took
her body heat and need
to heart,
while cold winds
rattled window-frames
and banged the coal-shed door.

The Other Side of the Street

is a row of faces watching. The windows are
the glad-eyes of the street; the gawping doors
with tongues held back will wag their say
when this is done.

                       They, give them their due,
expect her to be ladylike; but let them bite
on silence for a while:
she will dress, will not be carried down,
an ambulance is indignity enough.

This is like the last of trams, the last
Cunarder facing the horizon. They observe
her exit, marvelling. Each one of them can see
her clutch her handbag to her pain.

Fox Fur

My mother used to shoulder fox.
Dyed black. The brush dripped down
her front like ink.
                        She clipped it
like a bandolier. Snout directed
to her breasts.
                        It frightened me.
More than the brittle corsetry it coiled
round in her upstairs drawer.
                                    Its eyes
were globs of glass, unclosable. Its claws
like nibs. Flat silk belly
the feel of snake. My fingertips
imagined sin.

                Fox,
how many ravenous jumble sales
have they tossed you to
since then?

Light Sensitive

Glass is fusing, tightening its fist,
has negatived her sipped-at port,
his half-downed pint (he's out of shot,
a best suit nudging to the bar.)

It's Butlins years ago:
candles in bottlenecks, the Viennese Room.

She's facing what it is that kills,
leaning towards its summary click:

a thirtieth of a second in North Wales.

One Evening after the War

'Sweet Alice Blue Gown' on the radio.
The generations still intact. Not yet known
the news that put my father into bastardy,
stranded in a surname never ours. Not yet
the fracturing deaths that emptied out
the cupboards and the drawers, reduced
a family to its objects, a meagre pile
of misspent love.

           The song indulged lost grace,
an innocence of grandmothers before Great Wars.
We sat in tense nostalgia; in one
small still moment impressed by love's
impossible possibilities, drawn round
a fire built up to warm a man
due home from wind-scraped docks,
a woman knitting herself to death,
and reddening the cheeks of a boy for whom
her cable stitch was a secret text,
a cuneiform he could not read.

Home from Home

Home (ten miles from home)
is somewhere driven through
tuned in to music, watching the road.

On the left: St Leonard's Church.
I've travelled more than twenty years
from that once blitzed and rebuilt
focus, where all sermon long
I invested choirgirls with
too-intricate psychologies.

Yet theirs the first held-hands
in darks of terraced streets
and urged through flickering dreams
in back-row plush
of local palaces.

Church and cinema sneaked me away
from home, its smell
of oil and rope, of vinegar,
of chastely laundered sheets.

I wonder where in the world's warren
they are and which one's death
would make a sudden hole in me,
whose emigrating not surprise,
or who, like me, feels super-
annuated by teenage kids
and nibbles away a mortgage,
and whose divorce would put
a renegade if-only in my thoughts.

Education, also, exalted and betrayed.
I was the sailor's son who never put to sea.
I left the city like
the Cunard liners and returned
to find their red and black
familiar funnels gone from gaps
between the houses where I'd lived,
those girls become as vulgar as
tattoos along my father's arms.

Blossom Street

Memories and places. A jumbled itinerary
of journeying undergone.
                              It is myself
I am compiling, re-arranging a town
for reasons I don't understand.

Yesterday I parked, pulled in across
a residue of snow and walked
around the corner to a shop I'd found
last year – student cast-offs, books
in clumsy piles.
                        What is it that
accuses? I walked the length
of Blossom Street,
                              caught by a name
from thirty years ago, a terraced street,
ancestral place I'd never seen before.

But from here my father as a boy
was off-loaded to a Training Ship.
This is where the gibings start.
From here his ruined boyhood comes
spilling into what I have become.
This is where the sea begins its mutterings.

The place a memory, the memory a place.

My Father's Father

A shipping baron, high-collared and cravat,
with high ceilings in Rodney Street
and my grandmother in service, down
upon her knees.
                        Ledger script,
a best-behaviour copperplate,
red morocco desk top and gilt frames
of chestnut mares and clipper ships.

'In service' is the only part that's true,
prised out of tight-lipped aunts; the rest's
a daftness from the smell of brine
that's in my nostrils all the time.

My father was a stowaway who never knew
who it was that tucked him in the hold.

Sometimes I wonder at our name,
the fiction I inhabit and hand on,
and wish for my inheritance of fact.
Something signed would be enough.

Brown's Nautical Almanac, 1934

In this determiner of stars and tides,
ascensions, declinations, azimuths,
of navigable distances, beacons, buoys,
I see my father holding course
for the New World of his marriage,
myself two years away from sliding down
the slipway, dragging chains.

Here are his totems: polished brass
clinometers, liquid compass binnacles,
course correctors, sounding gear.
Here is esoteric lore: ephemeris
for tracking over sea and sky
by star-conjunction, numbered tides.
By this his bearings can be true
for civil days in port.

And here are hoisted storm cones
he must have seen: his rusty cut-wave
by North West Light and Bell Boat Beacon
thrusting in on Liverpool.

Seagulls

Father, you put seagulls on my tail
because I would not sail the world,
learn to walk on iron decks. For me
they'll never mean approaching land,
rope to bollard, feet again on stone.
I see them scavengers, rough lords
of rubbish dumps who strut on garbage,
dip beaks in waters rank with sewage
where the city stains its tides
blood-brown, mobbing wakes
of ferries, persecuting cargo boats
for galley slops; announcers too of storms,
they riot inland on rising winds,
spill frantic-white; and what they screech
is that the sea is only crossed with ships
or wings. You told me they were sailors' souls,
our proper kinsmen, that the wind one day
would lift you, horizon swivel, tilt,
the salt air scour each fibre. Now you hunch
at the wind's edge, unhappy with the thought.

Pongo, Old Lars, Billy Molloy,
handlers of derricks, expert winchmen,
splicers of ropes, indulge me here;
the time comes near for casting off:
soften the sneer in your seagull eyes
for those who landlubber, perch at the foot
of my father's bed and talk of old places,
Hobart, Valpo, Montevideo; recover those
sugar smells, apple smells thick under hatches;
and if he should ramble of shot nerves at Sicily,
tell him his suffering is shed on the wind.

They do not listen, being dead. Father,
the wind's edge is a cruel place. Their eyes
are graphite. They will not approach until
you fling them arteries or bowel.

Only once you spoke your heart to me,
admitted the sea's uncertainties, your fear
of being seen to fear, saying you'd
told no one this. I felt a hint of love,
a privilege. But then you turned
to face the wind again, resumed
your bluster, your codology,
your loyalty to dreams that carve
through oceans, anchor in the thighs
of continents that smell of sugar, apples,
demerara rum, where seagulls skim the wind
and welcome sailing men.

Corrosive rains, abrasive winds
now blotch your dreams and memories.

Too late for cure, disease has made
an innocent of you. You want more love
than I can muster up. The gulls are poised.
They hinge their wings. There is
the smell of sand and salt.

Buried at Sea

He entered the Gulf Stream
as if to ferment it,
give it body and percentage proof
of spirit. And all the briny molecules
rejoiced. Crabs savoured his coming;
polyp and tentacle reached out.
He dissolved in them. The whale's jaw
filtered him; the bivalve belched
its gratitude. The neatest grain
of him was sucked
through membranes of the silkiest cells
that scurry through unending sea. It was
his purest, his most generous act.

'Buried at sea,' my father proudly said
of his Best Man,
recalling berths and watches shared
through years and miles of open sea,
not knowing then
that they would tip his ashes out
in a family plot of rain-soaked land.

Ashes to Ashes

A gate closed, a gate between privets
palsied with soot. The breath
went out of the house.

Six feet of path,
two squares of soil
where flowers put on
brave faces for the street,
a doorstep scrubbed and holystoned,
four rooms oppressed by furniture,
a banked-up fire that smouldered with
intensities
of Father, Mother, Only Child.

Two dead:
a strong slow violence taking both
eight years apart. The same
green-distempered hospital, the same
bleak comforts at the crematorium,
the same rain falling.

And not much to show:
two bagfuls of ash we scattered on
the family plot,

              as if to fertilise,
as if a red rose and a briar should grow
to blazon all the violence again.

Dead Ringer

I've tried talking you round,
needing your thumbs up. But now
I'm past it and in any case
you've been dead too long. It's just
that sometimes at the mirror you
stare through me with something
quizzical that I've no answer to.

Easy for you, joking your way
out of almost everything. That night
I'm in the bath and you burst in:
'Swap,' you said, 'a tanner and
my owld one for that?'

Still can't get over your lying there
that way. A breathless mirror,
gawping and unfunny mouth.

Uncle Cliff's Lad

Well, cousin, you of the cargo boats and choppy seas,
blue-eyed jangler of gangways, who took on board
our old men's wilfulness, their crazy need for foreignness,
choosing the swan's way, to honour them, the whaleroad,

this is something between you and me: this is,
if you'll believe it, me signed-on and voyaging;
this is ship and sailors, chugging and on course,
gulls clamouring, braving all weathers;

and this is me too, after my Master's Ticket,
responsible for horizons, walking a liner's bridge
for them to approve, earning gold braid
for them to be proud, and sailing beyond.

Letting Us All Down

Won't speak to me. Draught excluder
wedged in tight. Rigid behind
unbudging lace, they've seen
my brazen foreign-job pull up.
Behind the door, folds of velvet drape
have stiffened. In an instant.

It's not enough to have spat
in the sea's paternal face,
shuddered at honourable muscle,
chains, grabs, slings, and winches
steaming in the oilskinned rain,
I've gone and made a song-and-dance
how love was treated
in meagre overheated lives,
how tenderness bewildered, angered,
how winds scraped bitterly
our grey streets.

        Can't help admiring
your spunk, aunt, the night you phoned,
in your pink slippers, breath catching
like someone holding on at panic's edge.
You'd seen my picture, smarmy in
the local press, read the cub
reporter's earnestness. Fierce
from long timidity, you dared me with
'Thank God your mam and dad are not alive.'

It seems love still stands
little chance. We always stiffened
over truth, drilled every nerve
to stay stock-still, prepared excuses
for reddened eyes, said nowt.

Myocardial Infarction

A hammer slipping and a blister
elderberried on the thumb,
a kettle spilt and a burn
fruiting in a mistletoe,
a knee scuffed like a toe-cap,
or neat capillaries red-inked
along the skin by a riled cat's nibs –
and he would say
'It'll be a pig's foot in the morning.'

Things invisible and serious,
dark-rooted pain, an ache that pulsed
the eyeballs – and he'd say 'One more
clean shirt for you, my lad' or 'Time
to dust the policies.'

And now here's me:
a pig's foot in the chest,
the planet-surface of the heart
blipped by meteorites. 'This one's
convicted,' doctors said
with their forever-word.

Part of my heart is dead,
gone gangrenous,
sloughed off and scarred. Do I say
it's strengthened by its scar,
is tougher now?

Statistics are undermining me.
And who's that climbing in the loft,
rummaging for documents,
huffing and puffing?
Who's counting shirts?

Three from the Ward
(for U.A. Fanthorpe)

I *Curtains*

Busby Berkeley stunner: a thirty-second sequence
of curtains swished one after one all down the ward.
I'm standing by my bed, a raw recruit, screened off
and hushed. Then trundlings and swivellings
on polished boards, quickly in and quickly out,
and final curtains scraped back one by one.

'Behind you! through the window!' next-bed said.

There in the open a metal box on wheels
and grinning porters rattling one of us away.

II *On the Mend*

Allowed up for a second day
of clattering the tea urn round
to beds with lungs that squelch,
arteries like fog-crazed motorways,
that scream their lumbar puncturings,
beds spiked with catheters and drips,
whose rawness keeps us all awake.

Word's ahead: I was *the last
to speak to him!*: cursed yesterday
for gazing hopefully into something shrivelled
that vaguely shook its head.

III *Parole*

At the end of a careless fortnight
they come for me, bringing shoes;
repossess my tapes and books, a still
uneaten orange. Angina in the next bed
writes an address in case I want to buy
his car.

    And bristling with advice –
*throw away the frying pan, give up
the Weed, don't get your leg over
immediately –*

        outside I bite
the granny smith of autumn air
and stiffen myself to meet the dog.

Birthday Poem for a Great-Aunt
(5th November 1979)

'They'll have to shoot me, Matt,' she laughs,
half-ashamed and marvelling, as if
to outlive's a naughtiness she has
excuses for. Today, at eighty-eight,
she'll jig the dust from carpets, flirt
her frock above her knees, outdance me
into gasping.

This is her compliment: to see me still
a hard-faced father's cheeky lad
wanting sixpence and his Sunday lunch.

My memory blurs on worthy things. It's
my teenage daughter who remembers
fires are lit and fireworks go up
on Auntie Sally's day – not me.

So now nudged into it and embarrassed at
how slovenly I get with love, I offer
something at least familiar:

'They'll have to shoot me first.'

Explaining the Death of Uncle

'Caught something in the hospital.' She stared
across the furniture. I had no heart
to contradict. The deep-stained wood,
the balding plush said let it go.

'A good man, Matt.' And I could not deny
the gentleness, his foreign Cockney playfulness.
The furniture required me not to lie. It knew
enough of love to put me in my place.

Same walnut clock, the cake-stand never used
for cakes, that curious poker and the radio
with fretwork cabinet he'd made away at sea –
all knew I'd ducked the funeral.

Old People's Home, Balliol Road

I myself have seen the wild roses grow
upon the very ground which is now the
centre of the borough of Bootle.
WILLIAM EWART GLADSTONE

This road I trogged to school down,
eleven-plus in fluorescing socks
and Yankee ties. The solid end of town,
Victorian sandstone with tall
windows, doors-up-steps and attics
for cramping servants in. I drive
through blackened gates to tarmac where
a garden used to breathe. And ring the bell.

Always at home, the Auntie Sally I ask for,
fetched away from telly to be kissed. She thinks
when I say 'Mattie' it's my dad who's come,
the same old hard-faced love, the same
old paid-off swaggering ashore, the same
old easy-come and easy-go.

She thinks when I say 'Uncle Ernie' he's
this minute gone upstairs, gone first as he
would always do each Sunday after lunch,
warming her side of the bed with his broad back
while she wipes dry just one last plate.

Wakey Wakey

'Somebody stole my girl.'

Clocks go forward into summertime,
faces altered round the house:
an hour's been lost. And now
the telephone has whispered more
must go: someone loved 'is dead'.
Today is Easter Day, that hard-
to-credit date with Resurrection;
there is more light to play with
and now the sense of being robbed.

Meant to be going on, not go!
two years off hearing from Her Majesty
or whoever it is that's keeping tabs
on centenarians; won't now be wheeled
in to 'hold it there' in 1991,
the telegram that matron reads aloud
in photos for the local rag; nor for
impossible interviews that want
amazing recipes for diddling death.

I know she'd slur and jumble words,
blur everything she'd seen and heard;
and I will miss the wisecracks wicked-she
tickled pink with once; know too
she's been *past it*, as they say,
for years: it is as if there comes
a time when time itself can die
before you and years-ago is just
another room in which your own dead wait
to joke of love and washing up and death,
a yellow budgie's jabbering along
with Billy Cotton's Band, it's Sunday,
there's roast and, expecting pocket money
and a sloppy kiss, I am there as well.

Waiting to Go

We waited shiftily – someone cracked
the crumby one about discovering
the town's dead centre – till the cars
the men in overcoats arrived.

And someone else – we were busy
rummaging for memories to stake
claims on being there – reminded us
how she herself refused to go

to funerals and said that this was one
she couldn't duck! The overcoats
came suddenly, spiriting away
our flowers, toadying us out

into sunlight, limousines, our first
sight, beyond touch, of her, boxed-in
behind glass: a ragged family
of women growing slighter, men more stooped,

more resigned to slow processions;
and glad not to be so senselessly
up front, they were looking forward to
tea, whisky, sausage rolls afterwards,

to catching up on each other's
tall tales and sorry histories,
as if nothing – each relieved
it was over with – had happened much.

No, After You

We stood about our opened-up family grave's
blank gape. Somewhere down there
generations level off and stratify.

Spooks in each other's histories,
we stood, disarmed of accusation,
confused at this moment of going

over precedence. At the grave's brink
we fingered soil impatiently,
thinking to bury everything but love.

The Minister

Not her beeswax coffin in the damp chapel,
its cut-to-size trestled stubbornness;
nor the four compass-pointing clocks
long broken, the municipal heartlessness
of that; nor the family-consuming grave:
nothing shocked so much as that old man's
sincerity, its uncomfortable comforting.

There we were in the town's back-yard
and the town going on without us, about to dump
someone we loved into the rotting ground
stained with other dead of ours – with this
quiet man tensing us with love, a gentleness
both personal and impersonal; his eyes
steadfast, hands unwavering, so each one there
sensed that something had been meant
if only vaguely and to someone somewhere else.

See You on the Christmas Tree She Said

OK, aunt, I will
look out for you
among the evergreen,

know you by –
what else? –
that squeezebox laughter
that never wants
us growing old:

just give me time
to rub the glitter
from my eyes.

No cause to miss
the divilment, my dad's
old buck: I'll
act the goat for you –
that's if
for some daft reason
he's not there;
and we will jig
the hornpipes he
was famous for.

Shameless, cuddling me,
old flirt, you'll say
'They got fed up,
they threw me off
the oilrigs, Matt!'
and we'll guffaw
for years and years.

And he'll be there,
your Ernie too, tuned in
to Billy Cotton's Band,
and when it's time
he'll wink
to nudge you up

the wooden hill
to do what you did
on Sunday afternoons
while I let on
you're dozing off
plum duff.

And I bet I click
with that blonde goodlooker
on tiptoe there
at the top of the tree,
the one in the skimpy tutu
with magic on her hands.

Black Sheep

Behind us
gravediggers
standing for
the briefest
ceremony.

In my hung head
I'm listening to
a back-gate latch,
a voice:

'It's only
your Auntie Fanny,
love.'

Decent Burial

Much overdug, this place, active
like allotments: yet each time I'm here
it looks untended, dowdy; I feel
the soil's resentment, its weariness
at one more raw intrusive grave; and know
that fireweed, nettle, bramble, dock,
if we allowed them in, would certainly
be welcomer than us. This afternoon
we're putting Fanny down, the Bilsborrow
black sheep, into the Bilsborrow grave,
she who acted over fifty years
its unforgiven innocent, its sad whipped bitch
with tucked-in tail, its specialist
in wretched deferences, who fifty years
endured a sister's (my grandmother's)
grand matriarchal righteousness because
some wastrel husband ditched her for
a plumper bit-of-skirt and left her with
a child that died. We hope to put our shame
down too. *Good-on-yer* goes the pattering soil.

94

Hospital Visit

My mother's mother, eighty-five.
Her hair like cotton-wool fluffed-out,
her face a smear. Only her eyes
(since nothing ever wipes off eyes)
definite, black with beautiful rage.

Twice in half-an-hour they seemed
to find my face. 'Matt, it's Matt,'
I urged. But she'd gone back
to glaring: something impatient
prowled the ward, some carrion-
monger she had to watch.

At the bedside, too, an aunt not seen
for thirteen years. 'Not since
your mother's death,' she said,
intent on estimating love.

And Cousin Marge, her daughter, still
searching me for la-di-dah,
reviving rites of sarcasm.

Three of us untrained
in watching out for death,
attentive to those glaring eyes,
the all-that-was-left of what we knew,
and anxious to woo back
something to chide our fear.

I drove home to a room
rigid with objects. It was as if
a retrospective exhibition had been staged
of what my life contained. My things
disowning me, just waiting
for purchasers to collect.

Funeral

Winds come sniffling up from the docks,
cold winds smelling of cargoes.
Some of my old selves are walking to meet me,
ganging up to challenge claims
on kinship and love.

         A spade is offered:
Take and eat: this is her body.
I crumble soil like wet cake.
The Chapel surveys its shipwrecks
through the eyes of a dead clock.

Is this where
the back-tracking finally leads,
to a foetal snugness six feet down?
Sprinkling dirt I seem to make
a reluctant promise to return.

Back at the house
they do not talk of her; they need
to measure distances by praising me.
I'm fed with cake and whisky pours
to let me know I'm prodigal,
the Scholarship Boy, head stuffed
with perfidious magics, home
for a funeral.

North Park

Uncle Walter kept it trim, a corner of
the park he 'had the upkeep of':
flower beds and bowling greens perfected by
the rain and his deft razoring, a man
gentled by flowers. The rest
was treeless waste no one reclaimed
after the Blitz: empty pond and paddling pool
and stretches of old scraggy grass
and cindered hollows where the bright Fair came
under cold rain to trick the town
with 'Jesse James's Bullet Hole'.
Like boys on topmasts, edging round
the sodden booth, canvas banging in the wind,
we acknowledged death and history:
that film-prop mummy lying there
as chlorine-green as the awful drowned,
the stub mark where the bullet bit.

Seaforth Shore Revisited

A vague perversity has brought me here
to routine waves. Behind me now
the town that tried to push me out to sea,
into my family's element. And literate,
I've puzzled out new roads,
roundabouts, flyovers, to come to this
old tramping-ground of clinkered sand
and fifty visible miles of sea,

forgetting how much sky
included me.

A gawky know-all girl avowed
that Turner painted sunsets here
dipping his brush in the raging fires
that slither into Ireland. And Sassoon
tossed his medal in this sea's grey face
glaring across the estuary to where
Wilfred Owen chased the winds
on horseback on New Brighton sands
before that war which trampled them.
And here we rummaged in the sand
for skulls and shrapnel,
scavenging like gulls to prove
our war.

Behind, behind for good,
the town's indifference. The rubble of
my toppled street is long bulldozed away.
Only sea and sky renew the thought
of freedoms brighter than my father hoped
wishing me to take his turn
over that horizon there.

Old Flame

It was there in her handshake again,
the something known and given up on
twenty years ago. Not softness
which can be tensed with urging but
that old limpness which always seemed
to be saying a vague goodbye.

The Beautiful Woman

She hasn't smiled, all evening
hasn't once betrayed
whatever sadness she's intent upon.
And yet for sure
she's seen a dockside commonness
beneath my skin,
the poet and the lecturer.

We're here to listen to poetry,
to children being dutiful,
handling poems they wrote for me
like jam or flowers at a fête.
She is used to this. Her sad
and beautiful face consents. Is this
an image for breeding's end?
Is she too dying of
a sort of emotional anaemia?

This green country's hers and all
its sky; Land Rover or Volvo shake
its hedges when she drives.
If I envy anything
it's the River Severn running through
her ancient land like a great nuisance.
Among its shimmying streamer weed
chub and barbel tensely hang;
and some of them have dropped their poise
to encounter me head-on
through the exact incision of a line.

Rolling Home
(for Tony)

In that shop
things stuck out their mitts
wanting to strike bargains,
get on with the job.

Hammers, brace-and-bits,
hearty saws, planes
that I'm cackhanded with,
chisels with more edge
than I can trust,
that scoff at fumbling,
my kind of muscle.

'Get yourself a big one, dad!'
The joke went home. I could
have had a son your age,
been less tentative with things,
had muscle in good stead.

                    Later,
in the glibnesses of whisky we
went staggering back through talk
of loves mistimed, ill-judged,
betrayed; unpicked our histories,
our same backslidings, prodigalities;
made trial of honesties; accused
this hard-faced Liverpool
which gave us all our cockiness
and guilt.

            And through the window –
surprised to see it there, Ford's
Assembly Plant, dreadnought on
the river bank too gross to launch:
you said, 'My father's working there...
this exact moment...while we booze.'

Something trembled, tautened.
'You'd like my dad,' you said.

Dead Carthorse on the Shore

Food is the dead we do not recognise
as dead. Prolonged into our lives,
the hacked beast, stripped fowl, drowned fish
inhabit meaning still. But this dead horse
the sea has dumped, that lies
in a depression which the tide
has vacuumed out from round its bulk,
is out of range. I must resort to images
to budge its weight from eye to mind:
a shifting, clattering deck, sprung ropes,
a headlong pitch of life poured out
towards the unhungry sea. Or some
old cocklepicker's drudge, collapsed
between the shafts, abandoned, borne
far down the coastline like a clump
of unhitched seaweed thrown up here.
Such images do not appease. Something
too solemn for explanation's lodged
hard in the heart, which not even
this powerhouse of flies can chorus out.

End of the Line
(for John and Mary Ireland)

The old girl's gone. An auction crowd
clicks among a King Tut hoard
of lustres, goblets, and torchères,
ormolu and Sèvres-pattern clocks.
Three hundred lots: gadroon, rosewood, jade,
porcelain, marble, and cut-glass.
A hundred years and more of *things*;
a shipping line wound up, an old girl dead
and at the breakers, emptied out
of house and home, posh vandals dragging all
the dignity apart, imperial plunder
that put Liverpool on everybody's map.

Here's a cardinal – scarlet Florentine,
an extensive landscape with overgrown
Italian column in the foreground,
a still life of summer blooms
spilling from a marble urn, a Cruikshank
Falstaff (chromolithographic plate
of a soused gurnet), an oval portrait of
a Saint (this was a pious house).

Men stoked furnaces, heaved cables,
loaded derricks up, and sang
tart songs in the teeth of the wind,
the eyes of storms, women prayed
and holystoned for these – gaudy objects,
gross antwacky foreign things.

In not one room a loyalty, no token of
labouring Liverpool, not a bit
of gratitude, no model ship or dockscape,
no smoking funnel anywhere. Just salvers,
claret jugs, mahogany dumb waiters,
and guilt, guilt everywhere.

A Few Words Before Going Ashore in Liverpool

She wants to think she's more than just
a casual jump; she likes the jokes,
the songs, the company; wants you to share
in your own loud generosities; pushing it,
dyes her hair peroxide blonde
combed up in beehives still. But then
trade's slumped – nothing like
the steady tonnage that once berthed
along this line of docks, all gone
to younger-looking bits of stuff,
to where the money's readier. So
when it's time to stagger back
to galleys, fo'c'sles, single bunks
she'll want to know she's seen-you-right.
Remember then – sincerity and wit. Her mam is
genial Lancashire, her dad a tomfool Irishman,
and there's Welsh tartness and Soy sauce
in all that stew of bruisers, gagsters,
back-street poets. And she'll be nervous,
satirical of 'posh'; maintain
her crackpot politics are 'fair'; spray-paint
her walls WE WANT THE RIOT TO WORK...GOD BLESS
OUR POPE-YE...Remember too that hardened by
goodbyes and quayside promises she dreams
of worlds apart and far-fetched continents;
knows all about mornings-after
when toughness counts its coppers, tots up hours
like gasmeters ticking, gaping into mirrors,
washing out her mouth.

Links with the New World
(for Liverpool's Maritime Museum)

They never shipped slaves here, except
odd ones to valet horses or to bring white cards
on silver trays to where fastidious women sat.
And yet spliced in with Mersey's scent of brine
and oil you sometimes smell black sweat
or hear (old seamen awed me with this yarn)
from pavements, oozing out, dark groans
under gratings near the waterfront;
or from the bellies of tethered cargo boats
faintly, but distinctly, catch
a babble of evolving blues. You can inspect
in the extant deck plans of old ships
that tangled masts at Liverpool
the merchants' callous symmetries,
resembling hobnails in a boot,
apportioning breathing space to slaves
swapped for sugar, cotton – moulting bales
trundled through damp Lancashire.

                                 Now
into rundown Georgian terraces
those slaves have sent disconsolate ghosts
chafing for room. The city's sullen conscience
walks common paving stones.

St Malachy's, Toxteth

The corner into Beaufort (B'you-fit) Street,
smacked by a sailing wind and the black grief
of a funeral: hinged-back doors of limousines
unloading, a coffin poised to slide, and wreaths
shivering in the air from off the docks. I had
to walk through it, insist, shoulder the wind,
dodge mourners, the stares of neighbours witnessing.

In St Malachy's Juniors, kids reckless like the wind
were set to writing poetry beneath the chipped-plaster
of a foot-high Christ, their age, imperially crowned
and pomped in crimson fineries.

                            In the wild street
the coffin was being shouldered, slotted into
Gothic darkness like a front-door key.

Ferry Crossing
(for Catherine)

Ten minutes' seamanship:
up abruptly,
like a fairground ride –

the screws' back-churn
lifting the Mersey under us,
swinging the stern to shore

and bringing us back
to this nervous and emaciated place,
Liverpool, we must call home,

father and daughter,
heads in a wind
smelling of salt – you concerned

to fathom my ghosts, those tough
old tars flying
in our wake,

and in that gull-crazed wind,
in a special effort of love,
you too showing me wings.

Father of the Bride
(for Catherine & Billy)

Smart and ominous in suits,
the groom's brothers, brothers in law
clutch cans of lager like grenades;

sisters, sisters in law
in crockery hats curl fingers round
champagne, fill the room
with lipstick, teeth;

and little lads in dicky bows
and little girls all curls
in first-communion frocks have got
the piano cornered and the cat.

The Best Man hates himself,
garbling by-heart sentiments,
telling a joke he bungles too – then
toasting 'Bride & Groom' robs me
of words that I have been
rehearsing for a stolid month.

The trestle table cache
is rapidly rifled, passed along
a line that's littered with
chicken bones and plastic plates,
confetti up the stairs and kids
stickying the ivories.

                    And now
in that same (vacuumed) room
with all the things put back
and everyone demobbed, the gaudy camp
dispersed, I sit, reword
that luckless speech to wish them luck:
my only-daughter crisp as icing for
her afternoon and the lad who startled
breakfast once five years ago and who
old-fashioned and abashed
asked her hand of me – given now
with the usual hesitations and a Dad's
confession to a serious sense
of swank and loss, walking her down
a gawping aisle, wearing a suit
he's sure to be uncertain in again.

Away from It All

Even here the seagulls come. Among the hills
where falcon, buzzard grimly range.
Even in valleys that belong to swifts
and linnets, where a rare kingfisher shoots
along the trout streams like electric charge,
they bring unwelcome white and grey.

Last night it rained, drowned out the owl, and on
the caravan's tin roof a medieval army drummed
itself into ferocious war. I dreamt
the seagulls were all drive back
into the sea.

Nothing so healthy.
Just two at first, perched hard-faced
like officers of some press gang, scurvy birds
with ancient curses on their beaks.

And then all day,
glinting white against green slopes, like words
hovering over blankness, wanting poems.

DEAD BAITING
in memory of Ian Tomlinson, d. 1982

Barbus Vulgaris

He'd take the piss.
So there's no sense in tackling up
with poncey words we'd never use
if he were here.

Living through his death's a swine,
his worst debunking. Here I am
a parody. I wear the look
he stared with when he *knew*.
Every ache and sneeze is terminal.

Since his last words – 'a long time,'
he said, (he said it twice),
'before we fish again' – a hooked
and frenzied thing has jerked
inside my throat. I've worried
oesophageal reflux and catarrh
to ten times worse, imagined lumps...

Now behind his back I'm paying dues,
thanking him for fishing skills,
while all I have's a squeamishness,
some luck with words, a sullen
promise: soon as I am fit

a double-figure barbel for his sake.

Caught

Spidering rodbags to roofracks, packing boots:
quiver tips, bait boxes, waders, nets –
this unlikely double act, lecturer and constable,
out to wet worms together, sluice them down
barbel's throats,
                    subversives armed and targeted
on Shropshire dawns, who slagged en route
each other's politics, gave God, love, sex
the run-around,
                    you brutal with dodginess in words,
me despising bigotries, word stopped in streets,
smacked in the mouth. Death wrongfooted,
caught us both.
                    And always now because of you
I'm wound up for the direst joke. Some afternoon
in August say, I'm trimming beech hedges
tacky with aphid or up a ladder dribbling paint
as tyres scrape the kerb and someone yells
'Are you on bloody holiday again!'
                                      I shear
through cable, fuse the whole caboodle,
splodge gloss everywhere, knees welding to rungs,
face white as when once I slammed that dead-
bait mackerel treble-hooked into your head,
pike fishing remember? and nurses rushed me cups
of tea and fetched a gardener with pliers for you,
or so you said.
                    Wayward, cruel as life,
you reel me out some line about a hush-
hush undercover job abroad.
                                      I gulp it in,
feel sidestrain check my wriggling protest:
how I stood among your colleagues stiff as pews
watching your glossy coffin jiggled in,
your wife, deathly in a black cocoon, propped up
by three bewildered kids; how I learnt
from a glazed stone's blackness with your dates
at last that middle name of yours.

So I'm netted, landed, sucking air. Some joke!
A cocksure constable walking the drive at any moment,
eyes quick with catches, the business of first light.

'Perfect' & 'Ideal'

Grey light shifting.

Cluck
of whirlpool, eddy,
water searching stone:

mist's lifting moment
of belief –
            the first
bellyflopping fish,
then a moorhen sputtering
over shifty sinuous weed.

Time to bite on those
two words we banned
as condition of casting
and first light,

wooing that instant,
the instant of *take*,
of lasering line,
rod tip plunged
to a thrashing thing
of love.

        Gravest words
never to jinx friendship with
nor the likelihood of dawn.

Sometimes

he'd try to make me feel
cackhanded, thick –
using too much lead,
the wrong-sized float,
getting snagged
or staying put when he
changed swims, explored
downstream.

        Sometimes
he'd ridicule the way
I'd stick with *one*
damned bait; would heckle
obvious things, like how
to thread a blade of grass
on the shank of a hook
to stop a bait
from flying off, or how
to handline when a hook
gets hitched to weed.

Sometimes I heard him gruff
with bailiffs
and yet forage river lore
from them – where barbel shoal
in winter or what bait's
been *paying off* of late.

And sometimes,
knowing the limpness
of Severn afternoons,
he'd snooze
an hour or two while I
persisted, legering
hypnotic glinting runs
where fish snoozed too.

Sometimes a wood pigeon,
to mock us both, would croon
Ole Man River crassly
all day long.

His First Barbel

Over drenched fields spooked with shapes
snorted by cows; over gates and stiles melting
in dew; rodbags snatching at bramble, hawthorn;
waders skidding on blood-red clay: that day
we fished frustratedly, dawn to blue-green dusk,
until he found the spot to cast in – legering worm
on gravel; and then his rod-end tugged, his line
became a singing violin, a fish kicked surface;
saw him lift, kiss it, sober as a man marrying;
into waters that were chuckling, ease it back.

And again, again – finding a shoal, six more
bronze and whiskered barbel crashing water
to his net; called me, set me down, showed me where
and how to send my lead, my spiked knot of worm,
wanting to share, wanting the joy of it for me.

Dead Baiting

The season before he died a barbel
straightened out his largest hook
and crashed through weedbeds scattering
white summer flowers that trail and bounce
the Severn's flow; then one day not one
but two shy spangling *specimen* roach
above two pound from a scummed pit
on a grey farm; and in Derbyshire
a snarling pike *well over thirty* hooked
on dead bait – bellysagging here between
his arms in this reminding photograph
that stares two pairs of eyes at me:

my friend's grim with doggedness and skill,
the pike's cold-blooded, livid with revenge.

O Wormes Meate

Bullying tackle through a kissing-gate that groaned,
bringing bait we'd dug the day before
to tease that *fearfullest of fish*, the chub,
we walked a churchyard to the river bank,
past tangles of wreaths clumped wet against
a wall, the earth still raw from burial. One year
of fishing left to you, a joke began its journey home:
'Look,' you said, 'some poor sod's being made a meal of there!'

Off the Hook

And so it happens – some years on,
a mild winter that bamboozles us
with flowers: upstairs, staring down,
I see a silver Metro on the drive,
a man, a clipboard swivelling out
and crash downstairs to open with
'Bastard you! Bloody bastard you!'

Like him enough. That clean-cut
solemnity, dependable public sense
of muscle, hardiness of bone.

'Mr Simpson?...Merseyside Police...glad
I caught you...we're...' – and for a split
second I do, I think it's him pretending
not to be – 'enquiring about an accident.'

Close up now it's never him.
I'm disappointed, safe. Turns out to be
my son they want: something has occurred
they think he may have seen. But David's not
yet home. Can he call back? 'Odd,' I say,
'you're very like a friend of mine who died
I once went fishing with...he was Police.'

Name? 'Not sure. I may have known someone
called that. Sorry to disturb you, sir.
Goodbye for now. And don't you anglers say Tight Lines?'

Convenience Shopping

I meet his wife in Tesco's dragging along
the son I'd promised to take fishing.

Five years on, the talking's easier. She says
'I've kept his tackle, loft's still full
of rods and things.' Among sensible rows
of ravioli, beans, 'I've thought,' I say,
'a lot about him recently.' In fact I have
been cursing him: I don't half so often set
the clock behind the dawn nor travel half
so far to fish. Accusations everywhere:
among sweetcorn, luncheon meat, on shelves
sandbagged with sugar, flour, between
glinting coffee jars.
                At the long checkout
I joke about *convenience*. The lad
is sullen. Is he remembering that crazed night
prodigal with leftover Christmas booze, she and I
hugged, howled terrifying elegies?

'Tell Matt what it is you want to be!' 'Male
model' comes out sulkily. 'Don't know what
his dad would say!'
                I do, she does, so does he:
slim, handsome, five years taller, *like his dad*,
and flaunting her reproachful eyes.

*   *   *

Bleak Midwinter
(i.m. Fr. Gus Reynolds)

At the hard heart of it, when ice
clamped the house and we were left
guessing the loft's dark mind,
keeping our weather eyes on pipes
for seizings-up and bursts, he died.

Here's his Christmas card: coach-and-four
outside a mufflered inn, the horses pert
Jane Austen heroines, the sky bluer than
a swimming pool, the snow
like him inspiring sprightliness.

'The Dickensian touch,' he notes, 'seems more
appropriate than usual.' And adds
'I still may go to hospital for some
surgical manipulation of the veins
but will wait until the ice has disappeared.'

A Trip to Millom
(for Norman Nicholson on his 70th birthday)

In Frizington, Cleator Moor, and Egremont
faith in landscape's undermined – yet I could
half believe, under sunlight, love
had workings there, that what might save us
was alive. I was scouting things that speak
of you: caustic glaring waves to west,
Windscale's stinkhorn towers, Black Combe.

May weather and that day Black Combe
all smiles. Millom, your town, the town
you've given whispers to, a brood of shops
and garages cheerful under it. There
in your father's house and yours, a tray
with glasses and a favourite Malt...

You've shown me how to recognise:
it's your making that I know this place,
at home among streets that seem
busy about your poetry all day. I've stared
through windows on to roofs and frontages
of thirty years' imagining, knowing
that home's a belonging – continuity
of slate and stone for you; for me
a kind of luggage dragged around.

At Death's Door
(i.m. Yvonne Nicholson)

I can't cope easily. It needs
more stomach and less love. It needs
the tenderness or gall that made me kiss
and give her flowers.

Bad day for visiting. An afternoon
settling its dust, a ticking room
and her eyes staring back
from the deep of a bruise too black

for me. Yet I didn't flinch from them.
I left chrysanthemums and brought home
what whisky flavours now,
a first last taste of waxen brow.

Send-off in Millom

(i.m. Norman Nicholson)

Closing in on itself, the day
huddled towards a still, a black-
hole centre. Crossing Duddon, we

headed for centre too: a spire
standing for steadfastness, community,
pointing the way for miles.

Parked, we toiled the churchyard mound,
shuffled in among a congregation
of mourners, awaited the poet's entrance.

Not like him to come in horizontally,
stiff in expensive overcoat, wheeled in
like a chef's masterpiece – unless

it's to give us Wigan, tease us out
of melancholy, take the stage again,
spout poems. And who on earth was that

in cocky dicky bow? a hired
ventriloquist for muffled repartee,
jack-in-the-box puppetry: 'Starting With

That Famous Poem Called *Sea to the West*!'?
But there were no mumblings, no stirrings
from within, no cheeky-chappy back-chat.

It all went woodenly. Outside,
in the hillside graveyard, we cast soil
that rattled like polite applause.

Stretcher Bearer
(i.m. Pop Baldwin)

Old man in white straw hat,
a blue-as-scabious afternoon.

Eight slight stone of him and bright-
eyed ninety-five. From dead

glass, broken stalks, and fireweed
fizzled out, from rummaged brambles

bringing fruit. He stopped me weeding
with gameful chat of Ypres and Somme,

of seventy Wounded in one day and duckboards
thumped and mud and hurt

bodies carted seven miles. And all the while
for dear dear life he held

a plastic bag of blackberries that dripped.

Vaughan Williams' *Lark Ascending*

Request this music at my wake
when everyone's half-canned
on Scotch and almost out
of dissolute affection and it's time
to imagine, to pretend something's riding
upwards out of very soil, something perhaps
(was this what Brooke naively meant?)
embarrassingly English, a longing so
sequestered, as in this, that only love
will know it: that violin way up
over somewhere green like Grantchester
and in a sky so keen and huge
it transforms meadow and slow river
into an illusion of forever; a day
of summer frocks and lovers
reconnoitring each other's mouths
and hearing – bowing it higher, higher –
above the scraping of the spades
this wistful speck of bird.

John Clare's Horizon

had to lie somewhere – hedge or ditch
exactly bordering on God. Wanted to know
where it lay from Helpston; found it

maddening – no end of lanes, of fields
where grass and leaves smelt strange,
larks babbled other dialects; wandered

mile on mile in search of it – an end
to far-as-eye-can-see despair;
settled on turning round, went home.

VILLAGE IN HEAVEN
four Stanley Spencer panels
(for Peter Street)

'Art is where I find peace.'

Stanley Spencer's Wedding Photo

Could be Arthur Askey – goggle-specs, flopped-pancake hat,
kecks hoisted up above the belly button – about to do
a Sand Dance in Maidenhead, while the uncertain Bride,
straw hat stitched with daisies, and the flat-capped Best Man,
like a gruff farmer on beery market day, are waiting for
I-say I-say to prick the daft solemnity. Only the camera
observes Stanley's wisp of smile.

Packs her off to catch the Cornish express and buggers back
to Cookhan to hump his first wife Hilda. It's the most ardent
day of his life. Afterwards in St Ives, when she
is scouring the honeymoon sands for shells to frame
a mirror, he tells the second Mrs S that God (the cld guy in
the dressing-gown) is Love; that he Stanley is a genius;
and if he cannot couple with the world, then at least he needs
two wives. In the slow fury of Atlantic surf, he runs ahead
scooping shells for her. He likes mirrors, they remind him
of home, the mantelpiece, vases of pampas grass, the clock
there under glass. He remembers domes of glass on Cookham graves:
as if the dead breathed bubbles of flowers. He yearns
for holy immoralities of gulls while grumbling how
he misses that old Cookham pram of his daughter Unity,
carting his paraphernalia down the stones of the windy pier
where he paints the sexless seascapes he needs for maintenance.

Towers and Towed: A Use Discovered for Lovers

Odd, this couple on the towpath, Cookham lock,
1889 – a green river's erotic undertones,
green lovers punting through swishing willows,
through swans, touchy, upping ferociously:
a couple walking there and bearing, like a yoke,
a boat-hook that trails a tow-rope to which
nothing is attached or from which something
has become detached. Someone is walking
on someone's grave. Stanley yet eight years old
when Jerome K. Jerome is creating George's droll
anecdote: how they 'got the hitcher...and reached
over, and drew in the end of the tow-line;
and they made a loop in it, and put it over
their mast, and then they tidied up the sculls,
and went and sat down in the stern and lit their pipes'
(paragraph) 'And that young man and young woman towed
those four hulking chaps and a heavy boat
up to Marlow.' O Stanley, if only you could have seen
the silliness then. Do you remember how dashingly
you separated the fighting swans with Patricia leaning
against the phallic bollard (what was that book
she had that day?), their beaks gripping like pegs
and three buxom angels blessing O heroic you?

In the Asylum Hilda Anticipates Stanley's Resurrection

Stanley's coming here again today awkward buses awkward trains
awkward Sunday waitings to Banstead with chocolates bringing me
his sweet ration and letters all the letters the week's great
celebrations Stanley's God says when the graves burst asunder
it will be Cookham and all the men and women will embrace
and copulate eternally mine has revealed to me that I
must escape my murderers the evil ones after me Stanley says
I ought to weigh God's words carefully before doing anything
but he's happy when I tell him what God thinks apparently
God no longer minds about the sex thing only Stanley wants me
just to write back dirty including dogs so what's the harm
if God says Stanley's going to put it all in a huge picture
him me Patricia the psychiatrist over and over eternally aroused

Get You to My Lady's Chamber

Our Wigan friend Peter, when he was able-bodied
(spine broke in four places falling off the back
of a lorry) once tugged a romantic forelock
in noble service down South, tending his lordship's
lawns and shrubberies and a dozen Spencer canvases –
'Had to keep the temperature right,' he says.

Among shuddering vine-leaves he caught sight
of a woman gobbling a tramp; left soon afterwards;
became gravemaker in Bolton. In the pits of
squelching graves, reeking of exhumations,
he brooded on Spencer's weirdo fantasies –
the polygamy, the clothes, the smells, the dogs,
God the Father in his tasselly dressing gown
prowling Cookham High Street like a holy
flasher, and those tombs like bouncing-up-and-down
Victorian bedsteads. 'All of them wankers,' he says.

John Middleton, the Childe of Hale
(1578-1623)

The local gentry gaudied me
to bring before the freakish king.
Tobacco, witches he was hot against.
Wrestling though
he liked; and I was prodigy enough.
I earned a purse of twenty pound
for putting out
his champion's thumb.

At Brasenose then
they went about my measurements;
full-length in all my lendings
painted me in oils,
while jackdaw scholars pecked about
my cowpat hands. I told them lies:
that dozing in a sandy place
I woke this size, burst all my clothes
like gorsepods in the summer's heat,
and stepping forth at nine-foot-three
met and hurled a fuming bull
head-first into Mersey silt.

And I was landmark after this
among the clods and fields of Hale.
But still my head undutifully turned
towards the river's runs of gold
each time I saw a sunset pour
its crucible. And sometimes too
the river glistened like a brand-
new knife, gulls threw their wings
like money thrown up carelessly.

It was then I longed
for marvels to be home among,
over the horizon's rim
where tall men walk ungawped-at.

At night I crawled into my mother's house
on hands and knees like some great dog.

The Song of Caedmon

And God said:
sing me somewhat, Caedmon.

I would have sung the mullet and whiting
shoaling at Whitby, the occasional porpoise
that breaks a summer horizon, the pigs
and goats poked into market.
I'd have had men listen
to new songs at harp-passings,
sung the wondrous windwork of gulls.

But God thought otherwise, sold me on dreams:
sing me Creation, Caedmon, the song
that's acceptable, that does me some credit.

So I the uneducated
was saddled with miracle; big words
broke on me, a galeforce of syllables
swept up from nowhere. I would have welcomed
a start nearer home, a local beginning.

But God thought otherwise:
work on my handiwork, carve it on crosses,
sing in Northumbrian the way the world got to
this bleak point of history. Sing to the mindful,
make me some worship.

I would have started the other way round,
charting our wonders, the wonders about us,
the disorder of gulls in a pleasure of words,
the glint of the mullet, the pigness of pigs.

Biographical note

Most of the poems in this collection have been carefully arranged so as to suggest an evolving story, a pattern of formative moments in the life of a poet who, born into a Liverpool seafaring family before the Second World War, grew up in the bombed back-streets of Bootle. It begins with evocations, in the sequence *All at 231*, of his parental grandparents' house, and then plots the route which took him away from his working-class background, carting with him his baggage of bitter-sweet memories: regrets, fidelities, a sense of betrayal, of how love can fail.

Progress is mapped from the emotional intensities of home in Bulwer Street, through the cultures of cinema, church, school – Gray Street Juniors with fastidious Miss Bingham's handwriting exercises and Bootle Grammar School with its redoubtable Belgian headmaster and Rabelaisian English teacher, Joe Ellis – towards university at Cambridge, then half-a-lifetime's teaching, mostly in Higher Education.

Matt Simpson's poems attempt to understand his particular past, to come to terms with it, and to create some understanding of what and where he is now. His poetic – and real – world is a world of warehouses, docks, cranes, ships, seagulls, salty winds, back-to-back houses, bombed sites, bonfires; of friendships; teachers; and of trips down Cemetery Road. The tone may be elegaic but it is not without a saving Scouse humour. Though it confronts loss and death, the poetry is ultimately celebratory. Dominating the work is the figure of the poet's father, a former merchant seaman and rigger at Liverpool's Canada Dock, who died in 1973. In many ways the poems create a belated relationship with this tough, gentle, jealous, violent, clever-witted and humorous man, an impossible dialogue.

After a couple of years' teaching in Cambridge where he met and married the German actress, Monika Weydert, and where his two children were born, Matt Simpson returned to Liverpool where he now lectures in English at Liverpool Institute of Higher Education. Over the years he has run a number of writing workshops and gained considerable experience with poetry in schools. His poems written for children feature in a number of anthologies and a collection is imminent.